# GLASS ENGRAVING
## — a practical guide

Josephine Majella Taylor, AFGE

Bishopsgate Press Ltd.
37 Union Street, London SE1 1SE

# ABOUT THE AUTHOR
## JOSEPHINE MAJELLA TAYLOR   AFGE

Josephine Majella Taylor studied fine art at Hammersmith School of Art, London (now part of Chelsea Art College). Finally specializing in the design and manufacture of Printed Textiles. Later became increasingly interested in glass, until finally decided to work full time in this field. She is an Associate Fellow of Guild of Glass Engravers and was founder chairman of the Sussex Branch of the Guild. She has since completed a second term in this office.

She has, for some years now, operated a professional studio for the design and manufacture of both Engraved and Stained Glass, for presentation and architectural purposes. She is a part time tutor of Glass Engraving at West Dean College, in Sussex, and has taught Glass Engraving and Screen Printing in the Middle East.

Techniques of Glass Engraving include: Diamond Point, Diamond Drill, Intaglio, Acid Etching and Sandblasting. She has held exhibitions in the Middle East, United States of America, Australia and, of course, the United Kingdom; and spends some time each year working abroad.

Taylor is happily married to a Civil Engineer and has two grown up daughters. The eldest working in Environmental Conservation and the youngest with an Airline Company.

The author wishes to thank those engravers who have lent their photographes and especially Tim Appleyard for the designs of the display stand in Chapter XI.

Copyright © J Majella Taylor 1991

**A Catalogue record of this book is available from the British Library.**

**ISBN 1  85219 058 2**

All enquires and requests relevant to this title should be sent to the publisher, Bishopsgate Press Ltd., 37 Union Street, London SE1 1SE.

Engraving — a practical guide

# WEST GRID STAMP

| | | | | | | | |
|------|------|------|-------|------|------|------|-------|
| NN | | RR | 02/97 | WW | | | |
| NT | | RT | | WO | | | |
| NC | | RC | | WL | | | |
| NH | | RD | 9/96 | WM | 2/96 | | |
| NL | | RF | | WT | 1/95. | | |
| NV | | RG | | WA | | | |
| NM | | RT | 9/95 | WR | | | |
| NB | 5/96 | RV | | WS | | | |
| NE | | | | | | | |
| NP | 6/95 | | | | | | |

# CONTENTS

# PHOTOGRAPHS - ILLUSTRATIONS

# INTRODUCTION

This book is written primarily for the beginner, but more advanced techniques are covered in later chapters, to encourage the student and others with some experience to try more and more difficult projects, until a very high degree of competence has been achieved.

The chapters follow a chronological working order, and it is suggested that the student becomes competent in each technique before moving on to the next chapter. In this way, over a period of time, the student should have mastered the basics of each technique. Having said that, some of our best engravers work entirely by hand and to master the art of stipple to perfection can take a great many years. Those who do not wish to use power tools would do well to master this technique, which gives a beautiful and mystical result impossible to produce by any other method.

As this book is mainly for those who wish to develop a rewarding hobby, and for those who will be working at home, I have left out three of the techniques which can be used to decorate glass. These are:

## Copper Wheel Engraving

This is a technique which is best learnt at first-hand from a copper wheel engraver. An apprentice can spend five or six years learning the techniques before reaching professional standard. The equipment is expensive and many of the tools have to be made by the engraver. Therefore, the best method of mastering engraving by copper wheel would be to become an apprentice in the engraving shop at one of the good glasshouses, or attend as a student at an art school with a specialist glass department.

## Deep Sandblasting and Many-depth Sandblasting

This technique also requires expensive and bulky equipment, plus a knowledge of air compression ratios and a good knowledge of various types of abrasives, their mesh size, sharpness and different composition. Different abrasives will give different textures and can be used in conjunction with one another. It would also be an asset to have knowledge of photographically produced screens and printing, as to have stencils made can be expensive. Again, a glasshouse or specialist glass art department would be the best way to learn.

## Deep Etching and Embossing by Acid

The acid used in this technique is one of the most dangerous and most corrosive available. The fumes given off are very toxic, and if the acid should touch, even lightly any part of the skin, it will cause serious burns. It is necessary to wear protective clothing and to have a strong extractor fan in the working area.

Neither sandblasting nor acid etching are suitable techniques to carry out under any but workshop conditions. However, the surface etching of glass can be carried out using an acid paste, which, although toxic if swallowed, is not dangerous if reasonable care is taken. The use of this paste is covered in Chapter III.

# Brief History of Glass Engraving

We do not really know when people discover how to make glass, but it is assumed to have been first made about 3000 BC. The first glass did not look at all like glass as we know it, but was probably a vitreous paste, which was used to cover beads used in jewellery and in glazing clay bowls. Later on, the glaze on the bowls would be built up by dipping and redipping the article in the glaze until it became quite thick, and then the clay would be removed to leave a glass vessel.

In about 50 BC it was discovered how to mouth-blow glass, and this method has changed little over the centuries. There is a romantic legend, attributed to Pliny, that tells of a group of merchants carrying a consignment of soda through Alexandria. In the evening, they lit a fire to cook their meal and then lay down to sleep, leaving the fire to burn itself out. When they awoke in the morning, they found their pots covered with a thin glaze, where the soda and sand had fused together. Was this how glass was discovered?

In this region of Egypt all the ingredients of glass are found: silica in the form of sand, ash in the form of potash or wood ash, and limestone. However, this romantic story is unlikely to be true, as the fusing together of these materials to make glass would need a much higher temperature than could be achieved by a cooking fire.

The first glass discovered which was actually decorated by cutting, is a beaker of the time of Tuthmosis III, shaped like a lotus flower, and dating from about 1450 BC. It was probably made by the dipping method, but its interest to engravers lies in the fact that it has the cartouche of Tuthmosis cut on the side. This is the equivalent of engraved initials today.

One of the most beautiful pieces of engraved work of the ancient world is the Portland vase, today housed in the British Museum in London. It is made of dark glass with a thin overlay of white glass which has been cut away by means of small chisels and engravers to leave a cameo design. This glass is dated from the the first century AD. and was the inspiration for the Wedgewood cameo designs used on some of their pottery.

*Golbet of Pharaoh Thutmose III. 2nd Century BC.*

In 1676 George Ravenscroft, an experimental chemist, was the first person to produce lead crystal glass. The famous Buggin bowl is diamond-point engraved by linear technique, and although crude by today's standards, it is well worth studying. It can be seen at the London Museum.

Stipple engraving reached the height of perfection in Holland in the seventeenth and early eighteenth centuries. The name which most readily spring to mind regarding the perfecting of this technique are David Wölff, Anna Roemer and Franz Greenwood. It is said that some Dutch engravers produced their stipple by tapping the diamond scriber with a small hammer. However, one can produce beautiful effects by a much gentler approach.

Once one moves into the realm of power tools, the variety of work that can be produced is staggering. They remove the barrier to polishing, giving a completely different method of producing light and shade. Different textures can be produced and used together to give more lively results. Much larger engravings can be tackled, and panels can be produced, using stone and composition wheels.

Intaglio cutting can now be achieved. This gives the impression of bas-relief sculpture, and a great feeling of the third dimension, and although time-consuming, the effects can be so beautiful that the whole effort is well worth making. In fact, engraving is such a wonderful art that both student and experienced engraver alike become totally absorbed by what they are doing. It is like opening a door on another world, full of light and excitement.

# CHAPTER I

# TOOLS

As the various techniques outlined in this book all need different tools, it is suggested that the student, no matter how eager, does not dash out and buy everything at once. Just acquire the tools required for each chapter as you need them, and thus the outlay can be spread over a period of time.

For all methods it is a good idea to have some waxed carbon paper to transfer your design onto the glass surface, as it is very bad practice to attach the design to the inner surface of the glass. This causes distortion of the design, and a fair amount of eyestrain.

## Hand Tools: Line and Frost

The first tool which must be acquired is a holder which will take all the engraving points that need to be used, both for line and frost work and for stipple. There are various types of holder on the market, ranging from clutch pens, which are a little light to hold, and which, when old, tend to let the point slip inside, to pin vices. The best pin vice is made of metal and has a screw and double collet at each end, which gives four different size apertures. These are very useful, as you can then use several types of bur or abrasive point.

The burs used in hand engraving are straight, with a slightly tapering working end. They are usually made of steel with diamond-dust chips electro-plated onto the shaft. There are various grades of dust, from coarse to very fine, and also scintered, which last much longer and have a very smooth cut. The scintered burs are usually made by distributing the diamond dust in a phosphor-bronze matrix. It is then bonded onto the shaft and moulded under great pressure at a very high temperature. As with other diamond burs, they can be made in several different grades. If you want to produce a very smooth cut, the finer grade you use the better. Because of the more complicated method of making them, they are, of course, a great deal more expensive than other burs, but you do have to balance this against their longer life and smoother finish.

The long, thin bur is affectionately called the 'rat's tail' by most engravers.

The other tool which is useful is an abrasive bur. These come in hard, medium and soft grades. The medium, which is usually grey-green, and the soft, which is white, and is usually of Arkansas stone, are the two most often used. These, used in conjunction with the diamond bur, can give interesting results.

Finally, we come to the etching paste. This paste contains bifluoride salts, which are toxic and must be kept well out of the reach of children or pets. In adult hands, however, it is quite safe, although normal precautions should be observed. If it gets on the skin, just wash it off straightaway and no harm will befall you. If put on with a brush, be sure not to put the brush near your mouth, in case you should get any on your tongue.

This paste can be used either with a Fablon stencil, which can be cut to shape with a craft knife, or can be used by marking your glass with an acid-resist pen, which will stop the acid paste attacking the glass. Another resist which is useful is clear nail varnish. Coloured varnish is not recommended, as the colour is difficult to remove from the etched glass.

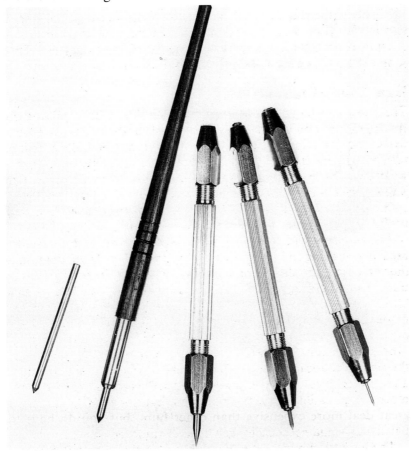

**HAND TOOLS**

*Reading from left to right:*
i. *Professional Diamond on Shaft.*
ii. *Turned Diamond Stylus.*
iii. *Micrograin 3.2mm Tungsten Carbide.*
iv. *1.6mm. Standard Tungsten Carbide.*
v. *1.mm Tungsten Carbide.*

*Photograph also shows standard pin vice, used for holding most points.*

## Stipple

Only two types of stylus are used, although several variations of these are available. The best known tool for cutting glass is, of course, the diamond. These can be bought for about £7 upwards, and some can be quite expensive. They can be obtained as rough diamond chips set on a shaft or, more normally, turned diamonds on a shaft. The angle can be anything from 90 to 60 degrees, but I find that a 75-degree angle is very convenient to use. The diamond, although a very hard substance is also a very brittle one and can break very easily. Care should therefore be taken with it, as explained in Chapter IV.

The other tool is made of tungsten carbide. These points can be bought in two grades and three or four different diameters. The hardest and most brittle of these is the micrograin, which is used by the most experienced engravers. Because it is very hard it does not need sharpening so often, but the disadvantage of it is that it is very brittle and will therefore break more easily. Micrograins are mostly only available in 3.2 mm diameter. Because of this they are more expensive and can be quite difficult to find.

The more common tungsten carbide tools have an additive which makes them less brittle. This, of course, also makes them softer, so they have to be sharpened more often. If using this tool, it is useful to have some means of sharpening it. The manufacturers will usually offer a resharpening service, but this is relatively expensive, and, of course, you have to wait for the points to be returned.

These points come in standard sizes, 1 mm, 1.6 mm and 3.2 mm. They can sometimes be found in 2 mm. The most popular size is 1.6 mm. For those with facilities for turning tungsten carbide, it is possible to buy the rod in long lengths, cut it to size and sharpen it yourself. This works out as a much cheaper method of buying the points.

## Drill Work

This, of course, means that you now have to buy a power tool. There are many on the market, so great thought must be put into deciding what you are going to do with it, and which you should buy. There are many small hobby tools, which work off battery and/or a transformer. These are cheap to buy and might do to get you started. However, they are not really suitable for any form of serious work, as, if used for any length of time, they will overheat and burn out. They also have a great tendency to be non-concentric, so that the bur in the collet wobbles, and good engraving is then absolutely impossible. You alone can decide whether to buy one of these drills, just to get started, or whether to wait a little longer until a pendant drill can be afforded.

Again, a large number of pendant drills are available. The points you must note are as follows:

12

**DIAMOND WHEELS AND BURS**                *Useful in Intaglio Work*

**SELECTION OF BURS AND ABRASIVES**

i.   For Frosting
ii.  Rats Tail. For outlining & fine work.
iii. Ball end, For Deeper work & Texturing.
iv.  Greenstone   for softer frosting
v.   Whitestone   and Tonal effect

1       The number of revs per minute; 12,000-15,000 are ideal.

2       The noise level. Some drills are extremely noisy, and if you
        are a quiet person it can be very wearing on the ears and
        nerves.

3    Whether there is a foot control or some other switch for varying speeds. A drill which only has one speed is not advisable, as several different effects need several different speeds.

At the top end of the market are the micro-motors, which are absolutely ideal, but which cost several hundred pounds.

Once you have started drill engraving, you will also need to expand the range of burs in your possession. A good selection would consist of the rat's tail (which should already be in the range used for hand engraving), a thicker straight bur, three different size ball ends, and some polishers. Also, to add to the abrasives you already possess, you will need a hard pink for use in the drill. The other very important piece of equipment is a mask which is recommended for protection against fine dust particles. An ordinary surgical mask will not do.

## Intaglio

We now come to the technique of cutting deeply into the glass, and to do this you will need water, first as a lubricant, second to cool the glass, and last, but certainly not least, to carry the glass dust away. This method of engraving produces a great deal of glass dust, and here the mask alone will not be adequate.

The working burs you need now have to be wheels and round-ended, capable of cutting deeply into the glass. These can be obtained in many sizes, from very tiny, no bigger than the head of a pin, to very large, for use on windows or large panels. The largest, which is easily handled in a pendant drill, would be in the region of 30 mm diameter. Wheels larger than this would need a much heavier and larger drill.

## Miscellaneous Tools

Other useful tools can be used to speed up the cutting, or to produce different effects. For fast cutting, abrasive composition wheels can be used. These come in various sizes and textures. The cut is normally relatively coarse. However, the cut can then be 'worked over' by using finer tools. If the finer tools were used on virgin glass, the depth of cut would take much longer to achieve.

Polishing wheels, powders and compounds are also very useful in all types of work, with the exception of hand engraving. The polishing wheels are made of rubber or acrylic in which are bonded abrasive powders. These range from very soft to very hard, and the choice depends on what type of polishing you wish to achieve. Polishing powders are used in the same way, and are applied on wooden, cork or felt wheels. The additional advantage of using this method is that it can smooth a rough engraving at the same time as it is polishing the glass.

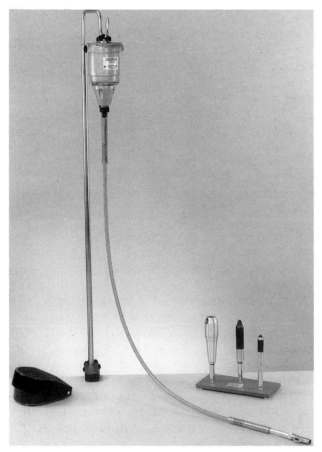

**PENDANT DRILL AND STAND**

*With selection of hand pieces. These drills can also be purchased with a fixed handpiece.*

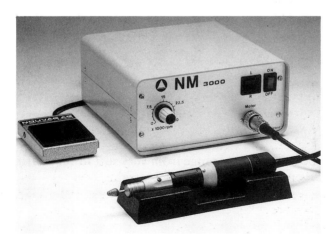

**MICROMOTOR**

If very delicate surface engraving is required, as in clouds and mist, an air abrasive gun can be used. These guns can be used with either a small compressor or bottled propulsion medium. This can be purchased from any supplier of air brushes. A water trap is also needed when using this tool, as the compressed air is very cold and condenses in normal temperatures. When this happens tiny droplets of water get into the gun and clog the abrasive.

Diamond tube drills are other useful tools, in that they can be used to cut holes in glass. This could be beneficial if making lamps, or as a means of attaching mirrors and panels to walls or screens.

For marking glass with straight horizontal lines (e.g. when lettering), a device like a retort stand is useful, with a clamp to hold a spirit based felt pen, which will draw on glass.

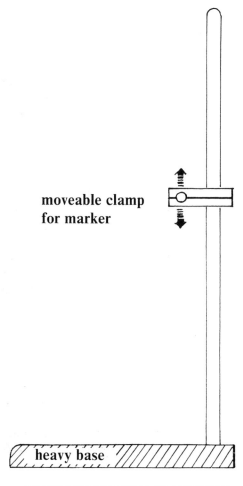

moveable clamp
for marker

heavy base

**STAND FOR MARKING GLASS WITH
VERTICAL OR HORIZONTAL LINES**

# CHAPTER II

# DESIGN FOR GLASS ENGRAVING

When designing for engraved glass, the artist must remember two important facts. First, that as a painter uses colour, the glass artist uses light. Second, that the material which is being worked on is transparent, and this creates several unique problems, especially when an 'all round' design is being considered.

It is always an advantage when engravers are capable of creating their own designs, for, apart from the satisfaction of seeing one's own design worked in the glass, the engraver can design specifically for the piece of glass on which work is about to begin, integrating the design with the glass to produce one work of art. There is also no nagging worry about copyright. One word of warning must be given here. If designs are borrowed from books, photographs or magazines, and used directly on the glass, one can be sued for infringing copyright law. Designs of this kind can, however, be used as the initial inspiration. This means that one can use the idea as a basis from which to work out one's own design. There is, however, a series of books which has been produced with no copyright attached to it, especially for craftsmen who are not also artists. These books cover a wide range of subjects and can be very useful indeed.

Before we begin discussing designs and working drawings, I think it would be a good idea to consider your working position and lighting. If either of these are not right, the muscles in the back, neck and eyes can become very fatigued, although you may not notice this until you stop work. Then you may find you have very sore eyes, perhaps a headache, a severe pain in your neck, shoulders and back.

I have, on several occasions, heard of hand engravers working on their laps while other members of the family watch television. Consider the strain this puts on the back. The spine must be in an acute curve, with the head bent forward at about an 80-degree angle, if not more. The light source, unless immediately over one's shoulder cannot be constant, as the light from the television set flickers when the figures move about on the screen. If this position is taken up frequently, it could cause permanent damage to the back and neck.

I am lucky in that I can work on an architect's drawing board, so that I can adjust the angle and height if I wish to. However, I realise that one has to have an alternative plan when working at home. Therefore, I suggest that a board could be used, set on an ordinary table, with the far end propped up on books, at an angle which is comfortable for you.

When working dry, the ideal method of supporting the glass would be to use a special cushion. To make this, you need a length of black cotton velvet. Nylon velvet is not satisfactory as it has some reflective qualities, while the cotton velvet has a matt finish. Make this into a cushion case and fill it with dried peas, rice or lentils. By using this filling the cushion can be made to hold any shape or size of glass, simply by laying it on a table and making the right size of depression in the middle of the cushion.

Lighting is also a very important consideration. Working near a good source of bright, natural light is the ideal, but in some climates one has to resort to other measures for most of the time. When deciding on which light to buy, several factors have to be considered. The ideal place for the light to be situated is in front of the engraver, but to the left. (In the case of left-handed engravers, place it to the

**WORKING DRAWING**

*This working drawing is for stipple engraving, but the same principle applies to working drawings for all techniques.*

right.) This ensures that, when working on the glass, one's own shadow does not fall on it, and that the maximum light falls on the work. The ideal would be an angled office or table lamp, or an architect's drawing board lamp. The bulb should be a cold light, as this is much better for displaying the engraving.

After the initial design has been worked out there are several things which one must do before starting to engrave the glass. The first of these is to produce a working drawing. This is done either on black scraperboard or on black paper using a white pencil. Scraperboard is the best medium to use, as the movement of the scraper pen on the board is similar to that of the diamond on the glass. However, it is not always readily available, and so a white drawing on black paper can be used instead. Everything that is to appear on the finished glass must be included on this working plan.

The working drawing is most important, and anyone who tries to hurry things up by omitting it may well live to regret the decision. Until the working drawing is complete, it is not possible to know what the design will look like on the glass. Mistakes cannot be rectified once engraved.

When an ordinary pen and pencil drawing is done on white paper, the shadows and darker areas are drawn in. On glass this would produce a negative (like a photographer's negative from which a positive print is taken). On glass, the parts drawn are the highlights and lighter areas, thus giving a positive impression. Therefore, when one does the working drawing as white on black, the effect is the same. If this drawing is not done first, however, the chances of engraving the wrong areas of the glass are greatly heightened, and it only takes a second of lost concentration to work 'naturally' and therefore make a wrong mark on the glass.

The next stage is to make a tracing of your design in order to transfer it onto the glass. The tracing is attached to the outside of the glass, and a special waxed transfer paper is placed between it and the glass with the waxed side against the glass surface. The design should then be traced through, using a hard point such as a ball-point pen. I use an old-fashioned gramophone needle, held in a pin vice, because it has a finer point than a pen. The finer the point, the finer the transferred design. To fix the wax impression on the glass, it can be sprayed with either fixative (as used in pastel painting) or hair spray. I just cover the glass with kitchen cling film and peel it away as the engraving progresses.

There are numerous other methods of transferring the design onto the glass surface. For instance, some people draw the design on with the chinagraph pencil or spirit-based felt pen. Another method, good for lettering, is to paint the glass with gouache and, when dry, scrape the design through with a blunt utensil. I find that a wooden cocktail stick held in a pin vice is the perfect instrument, as there is no possibility of it scratching the glass. However, in 90 per cent of cases I choose the wax transfer method as being the most efficient.

Setting the position of the design on the glass is another important factor. Most modern glass is put through an annealing oven, to cool very slowly after being blown, so that no stress occurs in the glass. When the glass is cool it is taken out of the oven and the top area, which was attached to the blowing pipe, is cut off, leaving a sharp edge. This is then put through a hot flame to soften the edge and smooth out the sharpness. The glass is then left to cool under normal temperature conditions, so that where the annealed glass meets the glass which cooled at a faster rate, a stress line forms. On antique glass this stress line does not appear, because the sharp edges would have been hand-polished instead of fire-polished.

**RINGING OFF**    *This occurs on the stress line of a glass, and is an ever present danger.*

20

Avoiding this stress line is most important, because if you touch it with an engraving point, it can 'ring off'. This means that a split will appear along the stress line, and the top of the glass will come away from the rest. This can be most distressing, especially when an engraving is part-way through or, worse still, even finished. If you see a tiny, bright speck near the top of your engraving, this can be a hint that the top could 'ring off'. Unfortunately, there is nothing you can do about it at this point.

This stress line is usually between 6 and 13 mm from the top of the glass, but this is not always the case. I use a stressometer to find the weak points. This looks like a square torch with a polarized lens and a loose polarized filter. The glass is held against the top of the torch so that the polarized light passes through it, and the filter is held on the inside of the glass and turned until no light passes through. At this point a thin yellow line will appear along the stressed area. Two polarized lenses could be used instead of the stressometer. In this case you would need a bright light behind them.

When working on a very heavy-based tumbler, decanter or bowl, care must also be taken when positioning the design. If the design is placed in too low a position, the engraving will be affected by the reflections of light from the thick base and will not easily be seen.

Consideration must also be given to the position from which the engraving is to be viewed. Is it an open bowl, which will be placed on a table? If so, the engraving would have to be worked on the underside of the bowl, and in reverse. Is it a stipple building on a goblet? Again, it is probable that it would be engraved in reverse on the back of the goblet, so that the engraving will be seen through the glass. This usually produces a more contained picture. If engraved on the front, the design gives the impression of 'spreading out'. On the other hand, if you are to work a coat of arms on a goblet, it would be better to work on the front. All of these factors must be considered when positioning the design.

Now we arrive at the problem of working an all round design on a transparent surface. Great thought must go into this, as without careful designing the finished goblet or bowl can just look like a confused mess. The secret is to work the design at a different level in each area of the glass, so that whichever direction it is viewed from, the engraving on the front area of the glass is either above or below the area of engraving on the back. This may sound an easy assignment, but in fact it is very difficult, and can take hours of work on the design.

The last point which I wish to cover in this chapter is that of perspective. If the article on which you are working is any shape but straight-sided, care must be taken at the design stage. This is not so important for flowing designs, such as flower sprays, but is critical when working on buildings, and also often when lettering. Even the slightest taper to the edge of the glass can make a great difference.

# CHAPTER III

# WORKING IN
# LINE AND FROST

As explained earlier, the tools for handwork are relatively few, but the way in which they are used is important if good engraving is to be the end product. The most important material for cutting glass is diamond, and two of the tools we use for handwork are made of this material.

The first is the diamond stylus. This is either a diamond chip in a holder or, more usually, a turned diamond. If the diamond chip is used it will have one side sharper than the other, so the point will have to be turned until the sharp part is discovered. When you have found the sharpest point, mark the place opposite to it on the shaft with some permanent mark.

The turned diamond points come in 60-, 75- or 90-degree angles, and although the 60-degree angle is easiest to use because you can see the point most clearly, it is also the easiest to break, as it is the sharpest. The 90-degree angle is best for beginners, but if you really feel that you must see where the diamond is touching the glass, the 75-degree angle is a good compromise, provided that you take a little extra care with it.

It is tempting to start engraving on old bottles or jam jars, but this is a false economy for two very good reasons. The first is that the tools which you are using are more expensive than crystal seconds, and working on hard glass will wear them out very quickly. Second, when working on hard glass it is impossible to stop the glass flaking along a line or in a frosted area, giving a very uneven finish. If you never produce anything which you think is well done, you will lose heart and give up trying, which would be a great pity, as glass engraving is such a satisfying craft. It would, therefore, pay you to find out where your nearest seconds shop is, and buy crystal from there to practise on.

With the glass firmly supported on the velvet cushion, and the design transferred onto the glass, as explained in the last chapter, you are ready to start. Prop up the working drawing in a spot where you can refer to it constantly. Insert the diamond point in the holder and hold it firmly. When using the *diamond scribe*, hold the tool at a 90-degree angle to the glass. The way you hold the tools is important because it controls the amount of control you have over the way the work is executed.

Place your index finger and the two middle fingers up the front of the holder, with the third finger near the working point; the thumb will automatically take up a position on the opposite side of the holder. Now, bend your little finger as far behind the point as you can, as this will give you maximum support. It may take a little time to get used to holding the tool in this way, instead of like a pen or pencil, but if you persevere you will find it comes naturally in time and gives you a great deal more control over your engraving. With your other hand, hold your wrist as firmly as you can to stop the point slipping, which you will find it is inclined to do at first. When you become proficient in using this tool, you will be able to proceed without supporting your wrist.

When using the diamond point, you must *never* cross a line which you have already cut and you should never go over a line which appears not to have marked. Although it seems unclear, it will have

**METHOD OF HOLDING TOOL**    *when working in stipple or line.*

23

cut, so just leave it alone. This is the most common reason for a diamond point breaking off. The more acute the angle of the diamond, the more likely this is to happen.

Now, with your arm moving from the shoulder, draw in your outlines on the bright side of the design only. If you draw them in on the dark side, the shadows will look strange with a bright line round them.

When the lines and linear highlights have been engraved take the diamond point out of the holder. Insert a daimond dust bur.

When holding the bur, a different approach is needed. The diamond stylus had to be held upright against the glass for maximum efficiency. The bur, on the other hand, is used on its side, so it must be held differently. Whereas the diamond stylus is just one chip of turned diamond, the bur is made up of tiny chips of diamond dust bound onto a steel shaft. The bur should be held with four fingers over the top of the holder, and the thumb at the bottom. Now turn the hand about 25 per cent to the right, (to the left if you are left-handed), and the holder and bur will be in the right position to begin engraving.

**METHOD OF HOLDING TOOL**         *when frosting by hand.*

When choosing the bur, a thin tapering shape should be selected, which bears the number 1B, but is commonly nicknamed the rat's tail amongst engravers. With this bur, shade the bright areas with very thin straight lines. These should be made by stroking the glass with the bur, and lifting it off at the end of each stroke. If you scrub the bur backwards and forwards on the glass, you will get a very uneven and unattractive finish. The strokes should always be kept very short, and a minimum of pressure applied to stop the glass from flaking. If the pressure is too great it will cause parts of the engraving to have a bright chipped look, as opposed to a nice smooth matt finish. The closer together the strokes, the whiter the effect. Cross-hatching on glass is seldom attractive, although this effect can be achieved with the bur, as this will not break on crossing lines already cut.

An attractive texture can be achieved by holding the bur loosely and bouncing it gently against the glass. The effect will be of tiny hair lines which will give a good semitone effect when used with frosting, but do not overdo it or it will spoil the effect of the whole!

The other method of marking glass is with an acid paste. This is not strictly engraving, but can be used to great effect, either as part of an engraved design or by itself. This technique is called etching.

As explained in the introduction, professional etching is carried out by using a hydroflouric acid, but this is such a dangerous compound that the etching can only be carried out in controlled workshop conditions, with protective clothing and other safety precautions. However, the surface marking of glass can also be achieved by use of an acid paste. This paste contains biflouride salts and, though toxic, it is safe for use by adults. It should, naturally be kept out of the reach of children or pets. If the paste gets on your skin or clothing, just wash it off with cold water. Avoid contact with your eyes and mouth.

When using this paste, the glass which is not to be etched must be protected in some way. If the design is of a broad nature, or is part of an engraving, the glass can be covered with transparent Fablon, which can be bought in any good hardware shop. The part of the design which is to be etched is then cut out with a sharp knife. The cut edges should be well burred down, using the handle of the knife, as great care must be taken to get rid of all the air bubbles. If there are any gaps, the paste will seep through and etch the glass in the wrong place.

If the design is very fine, an acid resist ink must be used. There is a very good acid-resist pen on the market, which can draw reasonably finely, or, if pressure is put on the point, can flood the ink over an area. This ink must be left to dry thoroughly, or it will not be effective. The design can either be drawn with this pen, in which case the background will be etched, leaving the design in silhouette, or the ink can be flooded onto the glass, and, when very dry, the design can be scratched through. This is a good method when working with a very fine design.

Other resists which can be used are clear nail varnish and woodworking glue. Both of these must be left to dry before scratching the design through them. If nail varnish is used, do not use a coloured variety, as the colour will stain the etching and is very difficult to remove. If woodworking glue is used, apply it very thinly over the glass, or it will prove impossible to scratch the design through it.

Whichever resist you decide to use, the next step is the same. The open areas must be carefully cleaned to remove all traces of oil or wax, as these would act as a resist. A mixture of vinegar and warm water is a good method of cleaning the glass, but great care must be taken *not to touch the resist*.

When this has been done, cover the open areas with a thick layer of paste. Use a brush as this will not damage the glass. Keep the paste moving gently, so as to get an even etch, but be very careful not to disturb the resist material underneath. When the paste has been working for about five minutes, take off the bulk of the paste and put it aside so that you can use it again. Do not put it back in the jar with the unused paste, as it now has particles of glass in it, but find another airtight jar to keep it in. (The jar, of course, should be plastic, otherwise the glass will etch.) Wash away the residue in cold water and take off the resist. (Wash the brush also.) The Fablon can be just peeled away, but the resist ink will have to be removed with acetone, and then the glass should be washed in warm water to get rid of the oily film.

A two-tone etch can be achieved if a cut stencil is used as opposed to the resist ink. Cut out the first stencil as before, and etch for only two minutes. Take off the paste and wash the glass under cold water. Then peel off the Fablon and put on a fresh film. Cut out different open areas, and again etch for two minutes. Clean the glass as before and peel off the film. It will be seen that where two etched areas overlap, the etching will be whiter.

The etching paste will work well on crystal or float glass, but is not successful if used on bora silicate glass.

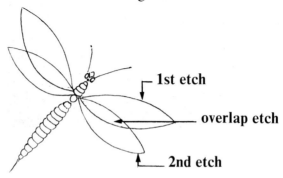

1st etch

overlap etch

2nd etch

The etching paste can be reused several times, so when taken off the etching should be put in an airtight plastic pot or jar. Do not mix with the unused paste in the original jar.

Each time the paste is used it will become thicker, and eventually will become unworkable and must them be discarded.

**SURFACE ENGRAVING**

*Christening Goblet.*
*engraved by the author.*

# CHAPTER IV

# WORKING IN STIPPLE

Stipple engraving was mainly developed by the Dutch engravers of the eighteenth century. The technique is one of great delicacy and is probably the most beautiful and mystical of all the engraving methods. It is done with a diamond point and also with tungsten carbide needles.

The names most commonly associated with the stipple engraving of eighteenth-century Holland are Franz Greenwood, Anna Roemers-Vischer and David Wölff.

The technique of stipple is much the same as in dripoint, where the design is built up by thousands of tiny dots. The stylus is again held at right angles to the glass, and this is most important, as the idea is to produce a series of small round dots. If the stylus is held at even a slightly different angle, it will slip fractionally, and you will have produced a small tadpole shape instead. This may seem unimportant, but, over all, thousands of small tadpoles do not look the same as thousands of small dots.

In stipple engraving, the tungsten carbide needle and the diamond point give different effects. The tungsten carbide will give a very fine haze, and then the diamond point can be used to highlight and emphasise parts of the engraving. Each engraver has his or her own method of putting the design on the glass, so I must emphasise that the method which I am about to explain is my own and may well not be used by anybody else. However, I find it efficient and so hope that you will too.

First of all, put your design on the glass, using waxed carbon paper, and spray it with fixative. Clean the fixative off the open areas of the design, leaving it covering only the lines, as this will make the stippling easier to see. When you have done this, check your working drawing to see where the open areas of your design (not to be engraved) are, and paint over them with gouache. The next step, while the paint is drying, is to organise the working area. Brush your velvet cushion to make sure that there are no tiny white specks on it — you do not want anything to distract you from the actual work, and such little specks can be most irritating. Make sure that your light is bright and is in the correct position. Anything as delicate as stipple engraving needs to be seen very clearly while work is in progress. If possible it is a good idea to work in a darkened room, as this cuts out all extraneous reflection, but it is not strictly necessary and so the choice is yours.

When working, many engravers use magnifiers. The best are the kind used in the surgical or dental professions. These are attached to a headband, and can also be worn by those who wear spectacles. These magnifiers enable you to see very clearly, so that when you take them off, your work looks wonderfully fine.

The blank you use for stipple should be of good quality crystal, with a high percentage lead content, (32 per cent being the highest). The softer the glass, the more delicate the work can be. On hard glass you will not be able to stipple at all.

First of all, take your tungsten carbide needle and gently stipple the whole area of the design, with the exeption of the areas which you have painted, and any fine lines which you wish to remain dark. The needle should be tapped up and down, very gently, against the glass. Do not forget to keep your stylus at an angle of 90-degrees against the working surface. The tapping should be so gently done that you hardly hear it, and at first you will not see anything, but persevere and do not be tempted to hit the glass harder, or you will make sharp, bright dots which will spoil the overall effect of your engraving. The idea is to produce a fine mist, not a blizzard!

When you have worked the design all over, take another look at your working drawing and decide which areas you wish to remain as they are at present. Paint over these areas and when the paint is dry, stipple the engraved areas over again, either leaving a hard line (as in some architectural subjects) or gently phasing the new engraving into that which you have already done. Repeat this method until you have all your background tones. Now remove the tungsten carbide needle and replace it with a diamond.

Carefully study your working drawing, to make quite sure where your highlights and brighter areas are to appear. Still tapping very gently, apply the diamond to the glass and stipple the brightest areas. When this is done, put in your final highlights and the engraving is finished.

Now is the time of truth, when you finally see your engraving as a whole. Wash of the gouache in warm water, and make sure that none remains in the tiny dots. A soft brush can be used for this, but if you are using full lead crystal be very careful, as it is easy to mark the glass by mistake, it being so soft. In fact, it is always a good idea to cover the areas of glass which are not to be engraved with self-adhesive Fablon, just as a protection. It would be a pity if a beautifully engraved glass was spoilt by a scratch across the back. Scratching glass can be done very easily, as even a tiny chip of glass or grit can do the damage.

When the gouache has all been removed, rinse it well in warm water containing a little vinegar, and then dry and polish it with a soft cloth. This will make the glass sparkle and the engraving crisp and clear.

It takes a lot of patience and practice to obtain the skill needed to stipple well, but once that skill has been mastered it will be possible to produce work of great beauty and delicacy which is unobtainable by any other method of engraving. So practise! practise! practise! Thomas Edison is reputed to have remarked that, 'Genius in one per cent inspiration and ninety-nine per cent perspiration' and this remark could well be applied to glass engraving.

Tungsten carbide needles blunt very easily, and need touching up on a diamond or hard composition wheel. It is quite difficult to do this at exactly the right angle, and the best way of accomplishing it is to have a small fixed lathe or grinding wheel. Put your tungsten carbide needle in your engraving drill and then, just gently touch the rotating tungsten carbide against the rotating sharpening wheel. The alternative is to send the points away for sharpening, but to do this you would need to own a good many points, so that you always had some available for use. Also, to have them professionally re-sharpened can be quite expensive.

**DIAMOND POINT STIPPLE ENGRAVING**  *Vase.*
*'Window on the East'*  *engraved by Jacques Ruijterman*

**TUNGSTEN POINT STIPPLE ENGRAVING**

*Portrait engraved by Tony Gilliam*

31

# CHAPTER V

# SURFACE ENGRAVING

There are many aspects to drill engraving. Again, it is most important to be comfortable when working, and the light should be correctly positioned and of reasonable intensity. When drill engraving, however, other matters must also be taken into account. The drill itself must be considered. If a flexi-shaft drill is to be used, it should be hung up just in front of the engraver's right shoulder (left shoulder for left-handers). It should be at a height where the burs can comfortably touch the glass without the flexi-shaft becoming unduly bent.

Manufacturers will usually give a year's guarantee with the drill and foot control, but the flexi-shaft is rarely guaranteed, as it can be abused, and the manufacturer cannot control how it will be used. The flexi-shaft itself is encased in an outer skin, usually of metal or plastic. If the shaft is bent in use, the inside cable rubs against the outside skin, and can become badly damaged or even broken, It is usually possible to tell if this is happening, as the outside skin becomes intensely hot at the bend, and should be straightened immediately.

Never wear scarves or anything around your neck, as these articles can become entagled in the drill and a serious accident could take place. An engraver could even be strangled by his or her own scarf. It is equally important to tie back long hair. The pain of one's hair being torn out if caught in the drill is to be contemplated. Some drills have a metal sheath which fits over the rotating nut. This should always be in place when the drill is being used, except when large cutting wheels or polishing wheels are being used, when the diameter of the wheels is larger than that of the sheath.

The other very real danger, when drill engraving, is the inhalation of glass dust. This dust can accumulate in the lung, causing serious illness, so it is important to take safety precautions. There are various masks on the market, and the ones used by glass engravers carry a kite-mark of the British Safety Standard, as being suitable protection against light dust particles. A gauze surgical mask is no protection whatever against glass dust and many of the other masks on the market are neither fine enough nor of a sufficiently good fit to exclude minute glass particles. These masks are neither beautiful nor comfortable to wear, but it must be stressed again that it is most important to wear them while drill engraving. Most masks come with instructions about when to change the filters. Don't be mean about this; if in doubt, change it.

Now that we have aired these important safety matters, it is time to get down to the engraving. Let us assume that the design has already been transferred onto the glass, using the waxed transfer paper. Look at your working drawing and see where the shadows come. If any are at the edge of the design features, the lines of wax on the glass, where the dark areas are to be, must be rubbed out. To engrave a white line across a dark area would be a disaster, so it is best to get rid of it at this stage.

Now select a fine bur to draw in the lines of the design. It is best to try to keep all your burs with the same diameter shaft, so that you do not have to keep changing the drill collets, which is a waste of time. Try the bur in the collet of the drill. (Most drills are sold with a selection of collet sizes, which can be changed when necessary). The bur should fit in it loosely, so that when the nut is tightened it will fit snugly and firmly. If the collet is too big, the nut will have to be tightened too much, damaging both it and the collet. If too small, the bur will wobble badly in use, and the collet teeth will become damaged and break.

When engraving the line. as you are about to do, use small strokes just touching each other. If you use long sweeping lines, the engraving will have a tendency to show tiny little chips along the edge of the line, making it look fuzzy. The drill should be used at about half speed. If going too fast, the small chips are also likely to appear along the engraved line. When all the lines of the engraving are drawn in, the bur must be changed. Now select a greenstone bur (medium grit size). With small, gentle, circular strokes, fill in *all* areas of the engraved design. At this stage the engraving must be as smooth as possible, as any work done over it with a diamond cannot be smooth if the base is uneven. When the stone bur engraving is complete, change the stone bur for a soft polishing cone. This cone is made of soft rubber impregnated with abrasive grit. With the drill rotating very slowly, work over the stone matt, until it has a grey silky look.

When this operation is finished, change the polishing cone for a hard polishing wheel. Now look carefully at the working drawing and decide where the shadows are to be on the engraved design. Mark these in with a soft lead pencil and then check your glass with the working drawing. If the two correspond, polish the marked areas with the hard wheel. The drill speed for this operation is quite fast, although still not at top speed. Keep checking the polishing areas with your finger, to make sure that the glass is not getting too hot.

The temperature at the glass surface can rise very quickly when polishing, and if not carefully controlled, can cause the glass to crack. When you have finished with the hard polish, put the soft polishing cone back in the drill and merge the hard polish area with the soft polished area. To do this you use the soft polishing cone at a higher drill speed than when it was used for the initial polish.

Now that your medium and dark areas are engraved, you must consider the bright areas. Look again at the working drawing. Put a thick or round-ended bur in the drill. With light, circular movements, fill in the whitest areas. Keep the engraving smooth. If it becomes rough or uneven, the whole effect will be spoilt. You should now have engraved all the tones you need. Only the highlights remain, and only a few areas should be highlighted. Change the bur for a really fine-pointed one. A number 1B would be a good choice. With the drill going fast, mark in the brightest tones. When this is done, wash the glass in warm water and vinegar, then polish it with a soft cloth, and your masterpiece is finished.

A word of warning about the polishing cones and wheels! They are impregnated with abrasive, so, although they are removing the white areas of the engraving, they are still cutting! Be very careful not to go over the edges of the design — if the cone touches the clear glass it will leave a small indentation and bloom on the clear glass surface. This is very difficult, and sometimes impossible, to remove.

**SURFACE ENGRAVING**

*Tankard: The Americas Cup 1987*
*Engraved by the author*

**CRYSTAL PLATE:** *Flight*

*Engraved by the author*

**SURFACE ENGRAVING**

*Using diamond and composition burs.*
*Crystal Box: engraved by the Author*

# CHAPTER VI

# INTAGLIO ENGRAVING

Once you have mastered the techniques of hand engraving and drill engraving, the next step is to move on to intaglio work. This is the name given to cutting more deeply into the glass to give a sculptural quality to the work. This, of course, needs much more patience, as the work is very slow. However, the finished work should be well worth the extra hours taken over it, if properly done. It must be stressed that complete competence in the preceding techniques must have been achieved before attempting intaglio, as it is much more difficult.

The hand and drill work which you have been doing, is like a two-dimensional drawing and now you must consider designing for cutting in three-dimensional sculptural form. At this stage it is even more important to have some artistic ability, as it is not possible to trace sculpture, and when the different depths are cut, the engraver must know where to cut them. The working drawing must be marked with the areas to be cut. The principle is that the closer the area is to look at, the deeper it must be cut. This is because an optical illusion makes the deepest (therefore furthest) cut from the eye look as though it is nearest. For example, if muscles are to be cut on an arm, the muscles must be cut the deepest.

As you see, a completely different approach to your working drawing is needed. Before, it was the light and shade which had to be marked on it, now it has to be the depths. I find the easiest method is to use coloured pencils, employing a different colour for each depth. The different depths do not have to be deeply cut, just enough to show a difference.

Before explaining the method of cutting, I think a few words about the equipment to be used would be in order.

First, as you will now be using wheels and ball ends, the friction of the wheel turning against the glass is greater than that of a bur. This causes the glass to overheat, and it can then crack. It is therefore necessary to use a coolant and lubricator, and water is the perfect answer to these problems. The use of water also elongates the life of the tools, which is no bad thing. The other important reason for using water is that the glass dust becomes immersed in it, and is washed away. As this form of engraving creates a great deal of ground-up glass, it is essential that it is dispersed in a safe way.

Of course, by using water you now face the hazard of another problem — electricity. It is absolutely essential that the drill used is double-insulated. Since the end of 1981 it has been compulsory for all dental drills sold to be double-insulated, but there are many older drills around, and some people have converted other types of drill or motor for use in engraving, which may not be safe with water. *So check that your drill is satisfactorily insulated before you start to work.*

Another problem when using water is that it is very difficult to see what you are doing, as the engraving becomes transparent when wet, and virtually disappears. The answer to this is lighting. The light must somehow shine through the glass, so that it shows up the texture of the engraved glass. Then you can see what you are doing!

There is a very good water bench on the market, but if you do not want to go to the expense of getting one, I will explain my own answer to the problem for you. I have a photographer's developing tray, and over the top of this I have attached, upside down, a plastic-covered *wire* dish drainer. The place where the plates would be drained makes a nice little nest for the glass to rest in. At the bottom of the tray I have placed a mirror tile, the largest that will fit in the tray. By shining a bright light onto the mirror, it reflects through the glass, and you can see what you are doing.

The only problem is that if a cold splash of water hits a hot light bulb, it will explode, so, to overcome this problem, I have put a sheet of Perspex (because it is lighter than glass) between the light and the work, and this appears to be a pretty good solution.

As we have been discussing working with water, it is important that you should be able to get it to your workbench without difficulty. Again, home-made methods are very effective. A plastic bottle of some kind could be hung from a stand at the side of the workbench. It should be suspended upside down and thin tubing put through the stopper with a small device for regulating the flow attached to the other end. All of this equipment can be bought from a local DIY wine-making shop, or from some branches of Boots.

The other method, if you can get one, is a discarded hospital drip feed bag or bottle. In this case a hole should be cut in the bottom, large enough to fill it with water. These bottles and bags usually have a tube and regulating valve already attached to them. The end of the tube should be suspended over the glass which is being engraved, so that a constant supply of clean water drips onto it.

When the tray is full it can simply be emptied, and the glass dust will go with the water. The toilet is probably the best place to empty it, as the glass dust will just be flushed away.

Now we come to the method of engraving. First of all, trace the outline of the design onto the glass, using the waxed carbon method.

It is unnecessary to mark more than the outline, as it is going to be cut away anyway. With a rat's tail bur, mark in the outline you have traced, not too heavily, as this ensures that there is no way in which it will wash off while engraving it under the water. With the water dripping relatively quickly, use a coarse diamond wheel, with rounded edges (a number 23B would be ideal) to cut away all the glass enclosed by your outline. The engraving must be as smooth as possible, so do not put too much pressure on the tool. The cut should be done in small circular movements, and should continue until *nearly* the depth you wish to achieve has been reached.

Now, change your diamond wheel for a medium carbarundum wheel of the same size and shape. If you cannot buy the correct shape, it is very easy to grind the edges of a sharp-edged wheel down by using sandpaper. Just put the wheel in the drill and turn the sharp edges of the wheel against the sandpaper until you have the shape you need. When doing this, make sure you use your mask, as the whole procedure creates a lot of dust.

Still using the water drip, but at a slower rate, cut over your engraving again, still using the small circular movements, but not too much pressure. Continue to do this until the engraving is really smooth. If there are any ruts in it, however small, it will be impossible to polish it satisfactorily, and you will have to go back and start all over again.

When this has been done, you start the whole process over again. You mark in the outline of all the depths, except the shallowest, which you have just finished, and then cut them all again. You then cut each depth in turn, until the whole engraving looks like a bas-relief sculpture. It is very important that each depth is really smooth before the next depth is cut, as, if you recut a bumpy surface the bumps and ruts become deeper and deeper, until it is impossible to get them out. When the engraving has reached this stage, it should have the small details added, and then it is ready for polishing.

There is another form of cutting, known as high-relief or cameo engraving, which is rarely done these days, as it is very time-consuming. In high-relief work the surface of the glass is cut away leaving the design standing proud of the background, in the manner of a cameo. The background has then to be polished back to nearly its original clearness — to get back exactly  the same is an impossibility, but the finish must be near.

When this is done, the design itself has to be cut, in the opposite way to intaglio work. The nearer parts must be nearer, and the whole design must be meticulously sculpted, to achieve all the details. All in all, it is a difficult and time-consuming task, which should only be attempted by those with great patience.

**VASE:** *The Undoer: Figure of Othello.* *Engraved by the author*

**VASE:** *Figure of Desdemona.* *Engraved by the author*

39

**VASE:** *Madam Butterfly*                    *Engraved by the author*

# CHAPTER VII

# POLISHING

The polishing of engraved glass should be done sparingly, as its purpose is to give emphasis to form and texture, and not the polishing of the whole engraving, as this will lead the engraving to take on a bland appearance with no character. Therefore, the engraver must be quite sure which parts of the engraving are in need of polishing before the work commences.

Many materials can be used for polishing engraved glass, and these will be discussed in this chapter. Before we start, however, it is most important to understand that whichever material you choose to polish with, you are still cutting the glass. It is therefore essential to stay within the confines of the engraving. If the clear glass is touched while polishing is in progress, the clear glass will be marked.

After polishing, the engraving should have a silky sheen, so it is important to stop working on the glass at the correct moment. Overpolishing will result in an oily appearance, which is most unpleasant.

There are a great number of rubber wheels which are impregnated with grits of various grades, and they are generally quite good for doing quick work. However, they do not give the delicate finish which one can achieve with polishing grits. Also, the polishing grits are applied on wood, cork or felt wheels, which help to smooth the finish on the engraving at the same time as polishing.

First of all, we will consider the rubber polishers. These come as wheels, cones, or are ball-ended, and are impregnated with grits. They need no lubrication in use (although care should be taken to ensure that the glass does not overheat while using them) and so are very easy to use. Generally, the harder the material of which the wheel is made, the darker the polish which you can achieve. If they are very bendy, they usually give a more subtle polish. If you are using the cones, the drill speed must be kept to a minimum as the ends of the cones are inclined to whip out, making it difficult to get a precise mark on the glass.

When polishing, the speed of the drill is critical to the effect achieved, and, in general, for delicate polishing the drill should be rotating at a very slow speed. If you have a drill which cannot rotate slowly, delicate polishing will not be possible. The harder wheels, for a heavy polish, can be used at a higher speed, but I must admit I never polish at high speeds. The effect is not attractive, and you cannot achieve any blending of tone.

As already mentioned, the slightest movement of the drill outside the engraved area will mark the glass. A degree of protection can be given by covering the entire glass with clear self-adhesive Fablon and by cutting out the engraved area with a sharp craft knife. If the polishing wheel then goes over the edge of the engraved area, you have at least a chance of the clear glass being undamaged.

The traditional method of polishing is done with different grades of abrasive substances suspended in oil or water. Here it is equally important not to damage the unengraved glass, and some form of protection, such as that mentioned above, is desirable.

The density of the abrasive is measured in mesh sizes, the lower the number, the coarser the grit. There are many different abrasives, but I like carborundum or aluminium oxide. Cerium oxide or tin oxide can be used for final polishing, when a polish close to the original surface clarity of the glass is required.

As I mentioned earlier, wheels of wood, cork and felt are used. The cork and wooden wheels will probably have to be made by the engraver. The felt wheels are easy to find and can be bought from craft or DIY shops. When making wooden wheels, the easiest way is to use dowling cut into discs. For the cork wheels, either a cork table mat can be cut or the top portion of a sparkling wine cork can be used. The bottom parts of these corks and the corks from still wine bottles, are not suitable. Cobbler's leather is another good material from which to make polishing wheels, but unfortunately, it is quite difficult to find.

The easiest way of making wheels is to cut a rough round shape of the necessary sizes and then trim the edge to as nearly circular as you can. Measure the diameter of the wheel and, on a piece of stiff paper or card, draw a square of the same size. Draw lines from corner to corner; so that the lines cross is the centre. Place the card directly over the wheel and punch through the centre of the card with something sharp. This will mark the centre of your wheel. When you have done this, attach it to your mandrel (spindle) and place it in the drill. Run the edge of the wheel flat against a piece of coarse sandpaper until the wheel is running true. This will produce a lot of wood dust, so wear your mask. When the wheel is running true, it is then ready for the edges to be shaped. This should be done on fine sandpaper. When the wheel is finished, it should be left soaking in fine oil for a few hours and then blotted dry. This is done so that the abrasive clings to and impregnates the wheel more quickly, which

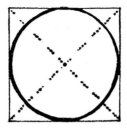

**to find centre of wheel: cut card of same size, mark centre as shown and then stick wheel to back of card and punch through with sharp instrument.**

makes for ease of use. Well-worn wheels are generally easier to use as they have been 'broken in'.

Now we come to the method for polishing the glass. Copper wheel engravers cut the glass with abrasive suspended in oil, so the engraving has a beautiful sheen. When cutting with diamond wheels and water that sheen is missing, so the first thing to be done is to achieve it. To do this, use grit of about 300 mesh size. Mix it into a slurry with light oil (I use refined linseed oil) and then using your round-edged wooden wheel, polish the engraving with the slurry. Again, use small circular movements without much pressure. This is a very messy job, so make sure that both you and your surroundings are well protected from oily splashes.

To find out how the polishing is going, the slurry will have to be washed off with warm water. Never rub it off, for if you do the grains of abrasive are bound to scratch the glass. You may have to do this several times, as it is most important that you do not overpolish. When all the chalkiness has disappeared, and a gentle sheen has taken its place, you are ready for the next step.

When you are ready to change the grit for the second polish, you must clear away *all* the slurry and dry abrasive you have been using. Clean down the working surface also, for, when using the finer grit, it is most important that not one grain of the coarser abrasive remains. The wheels used for each grade of abrasive mixture should be kept in separate boxes, with the grade marked clearly on the lid.

The glass to be polished should now be studied carefully. The completed first stage may be seen to be not entirely satisfactory and it may be desirable to go over the whole design again. If overpolished, it will have to be matted out again and repolished. However, assuming that it is just right, prepare for the second polish. First of all, decide where this is to be done. You may want a slightly darker area to emphasise the shape, or perhaps the natural markings on an animal or plant. When you have decided where to work, it is a good idea to mark the outline of the area to be polished with a very fine spirit-based pen, which can easily be removed. When deciding where the second polish is to go, remember that any part of the glass on which you wish to put the final darkest polish, must first have had the second polish.

Mix up some finer abrasive (mesh size 400 is good) and, using the cork wheel, polish the desired area, again checking from time to time, to see how you are progressing. When you have achieved the desired effect, wash the glass and clear away all abrasives and wheels used at this stage. You may, at this point, decide that the engraving is finished, and that there is nothing more you wish to do to it.

If this is not the case, we now come to the final polishing of the darkest areas of the engraving. Perhaps you want to polish clear the eye of an animal, or very dark markings on a bird. For this you will need your felt wheel, or, if the area is small, a matchstick or cocktail stick with the ends rounded off. This time, use the cerium oxide. Mix it to a creamy paste with water, and apply it to the desired area. Again, use small circular movements. This time be careful; the water will evaporate quickly in the heat generated by the friction of the wheel against the glass. The dry abrasive may scratch your carefully prepared area, or, worse still, the glass may crack if it gets too hot, so keep it damp at all times when you are working on it. Apply more slurry or more water as needed, but do not let the abrasive become dry. When you have finished, take off the protective Fablon and wash the glass in a mixture of warm water and vinegar. Dry it with a soft cloth, and you should be holding a beautifully engraved glass.

# Minimizing Mistakes

The other area where polishing can help is in minimizing mistakes. The most common of these happen when lettering. With most other engravings the design can be altered slightly to camouflage the error. It must be stressed that it is not possible to remove the mistake completely, because of the fact that no matter what medium you use on the glass, it is still cutting. So, even if you remove the mistake perfectly, which is not easy, you are still left with a small concave mark on the glass, which will show if the light hits it at an angle.

Let us assume that you have spelt a word or a name incorrectly, and there is just one letter wrong near the end. First of all, take a medium abrasive stone, (a greenstone). With small circular movements, but not much pressure, the glass over the wrong letter should be ground gently away. The surrounding glass should also be removed, as there will be a dishing effect if only the small amount of glass round the error is removed. The drill should be rotating slowly. When the letter has disappeared and the matting has tapered off to clear glass, take a flat rod of glass for the next stage. The rod is made by cutting a strip of glass and smoothing the edges. The end should be chamfered (see illustration). Mix carborundum powder and water to a creamy consistency and start polishing the glass, using this mixture and the glass rod. Gently work over the matted area by hand, until all signs of the cutting wheel are erased. This can take quite a long time, so be prepared to be patient. When you have a very smooth surface, mix up a cream of pumice powder and water and, with the cork wheel, buff the area until it is very smooth and completely clear, apart from the slight bloom which will be on the glass. Great care should be taken while doing this, as the water will evaporate quickly in the heat generated, and this can crack the glass.

For the final polish to remove the bloom, mix ceruim oxide and water to a liquid creamy consistency, and use a felt wheel to buff the glass using the drill at a very slow speed. The same caution is needed as before with regard to the overheating of the glass.

For the final polish to remove the bloom, mix cerium oxide and medium impregnated rubber polishing wheel. The same care must be taken to avoid dishing in the glass, and the bloom is removed as above.

In cases of large errors or errors on valuable glass, it is advisable to to seek the services of a specialist company for their removal.

**glass rod for hand polishing.**

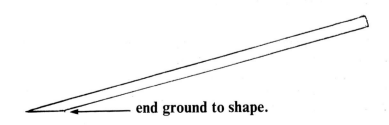

**end ground to shape.**

# CHAPTER VIII

# LETTERING ON GLASS

Lettering is the most unforgiving form of design to engrave on glass. When pictures and designs go slightly wrong, it is always possible to change the design a little, or to camouflage it in some way. When lettering goes wrong, it is wrong, and there is very little you can do about it. Even a downstroke which is slightly too wide, sticks out like a sore thumb.

It is obviously a good thing if you are already good at calligraphy. If you have no idea about the structure of letters, the whole procedure becomes impossible. Traced letters have a very dead look about them; they lack spontaneity.

There are a good many books on calligraphy which can be studied. These will explain the different spacing which different letters need, and how they will look when they are together. It is well worth the time spent studying these books or attending a calligraphy class, as, in nine times out of ten, glass is for presentation purposes, and the design will have to incorporate lettering, which will have to be engraved on a curved surface.

If designing on the flat, as opposed to directly on the glass, it is important to understand that, apart from goblets with dead straight sides, there will always be a curve at the base of the lettering. Even on glasses where the flair is hardly noticeable, the curve is still there. To make sure the correct curve is achieved, the following procedure can be followed.

Cut a piece of tracing paper to work on. Using some method of holding the pen firmly at the correct height (I use my retort stand), turn the glass round so that a straight line is drawn round the glass. One should be drawn where the base of the lettering is to be, one at the top of the lower-case letters, and one at the top of the upper-case letters. Now tape the tracing paper over the glass, and carefully trace the lines through onto the paper. When the paper is taken off the glass, you will find that the lines on the paper are curved. Leave the drawn lines on the glass, as they can be used to position your design when you are ready to transfer it onto the glass.

# DIAGRAM: EXPLAINING DESIGN CURVATURE

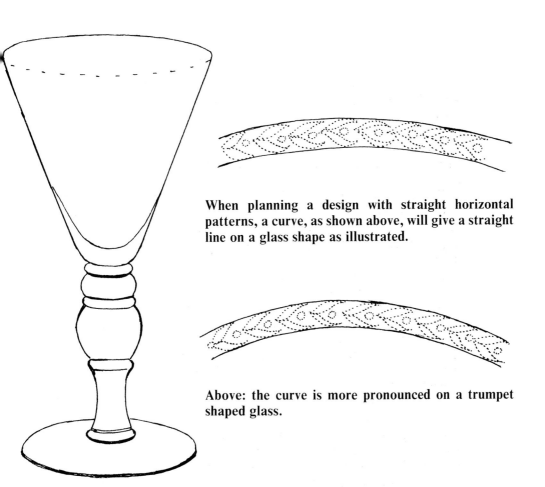

When planning a design with straight horizontal patterns, a curve, as shown above, will give a straight line on a glass shape as illustrated.

Above: the curve is more pronounced on a trumpet shaped glass.

# Dense Lettering: Drill Engraving and Etching

This type of lettering is the one used in most instances, as it is white and very easy to read. It is also probably the easiest to do, as long as you are careful about the constancy of line measurement. The other important point is the finish of the matted letters. They must be very smooth. If roughly done they look very amateur and scratchy. When doing this type of lettering I usually engrave only the outside line of the letter, and then gradually thicken it from the inside at the appropriate points. This enables the engraver to stop when the required thickness of line has been achieved, and is the best way to keep the letters constant. If the outlines of the letters are engraved first, with the intention of filling them in, constant width of line is much more difficult.

Firstly, the outlines must be engraved to exactly the correct width. If the drill slips a fraction of a millimetre while doing this, the line must be thickened to cover the mark, with the result that it shows as one thick letter amongst the others, or else all the letters will have to be thickened to match, and this changes their design. Also, care must be taken to ensure that there is no slight chipping of the outline, or the same problem occurs.

When etching, one can outline the letters with a fine bur. Again, care must be taken not to chip the glass on *either* side of the cut line, as etching is not as dense as frosting, and the chipping will show through. When the line is cut, clear Fablon should be stretched over the area of the proposed etch, and quite a bit beyond. Any etching paste which inadvertently gets on the glass will etch it very quickly. Now, with a sharp craft knife, cut out the letters. Bur down the edges of the Fablon where you have cut it, to make sure that there are no little air bubbles, where the paste could creep under to ruin your glass. Spread the etching paste thickly over the area you want to etch. Leave it on for about four minutes, agitating it gently. When the time is up, remove the excess paste and return it to the appropriate pot. Wash the remainder off in cold water and remove the stencil. Dry with a soft cloth, and your etching is finished.

If you do not want to have an engraved line around your etching, the letters can be drawn with a felt-tip pen, and then covered with Fablon and cut out. The exposed glass should then be cleaned down with spirit, as the pen could possibly act as a resist. The etching then proceeds as before.

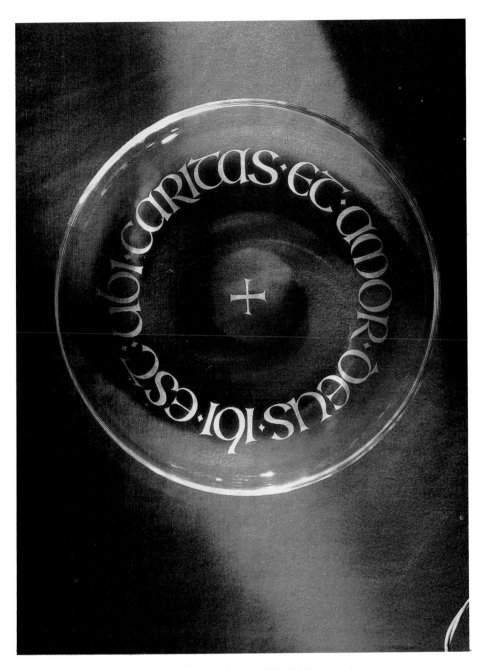

**SURFACE LETTERING**

*In classic form.*
*Crystal Plate. Engraved by Tony Gilliam*

# Outline Lettering

This form of lettering is quite difficult to do well, but when done correctly, it is beautiful to behold. This time, only the outline of the lettering is engraved, with all the attendant problems discussed in the last section. This time, care must be taken on both the outside and the inside of each line, to avoid chipping, as there is no frosting to cover up any small error. Before the engraving begins, it is necessary to decide whether you want the outlining lines to be all the same widths or whether you want them to be different widths at different parts of the letter. This decision is very important, as the character of the letters will be quite different from each other.

When the lettering design is transferred to the glass, by whichever method you have chosen, put a very fine bur into your drill. Make sure the drill is running concentrically, as, if not, the bur will hit the glass unevenly, and chipping will be unavoidable. Run the drill slowly, as this will also help you to avoid chipping the line. When all the outlines have been engraved, change the bur for a small round-headed one, and go over the lines you have already cut. If you use a water drip to do this you will manage a cleaner, smoother cut. The ball end will bite deeper into the glass, giving you a smooth, deep line. If you have decided to thicken your outline in places, run the ball end against the side of the cut you have already made, until the desired thickness has been achieved. Do not forget to keep the thickness you have decided on the same in every letter.

# Flowing Lettering

The lettering will be either italic or copperplate, and some practice on the flat is recommended before it is attempted on a curved surface. The lettering is frequently on a slant, although this is not a hard and fast rule. It is important to ensure that all the letters are on the same slant, or the finished engraving will look very untidy indeed. For this type of lettering, it is suggested that the dense technique is best, as the outline technique is more suitable for lettering such as Roman or Sans Gill.

The beginner would be wise to design on paper first, as getting the slant right can be tricky. Start off by getting the horizontal curve of the lettering correct, as described at the beginning of this chapter. Draw a parallel line above the top line which denotes the top of the upper-case letters. Now, on the lowest line, mark the areas where your letters are to begin. For the next step, you will need a protractor. Decide at what angle you want your lettering to lie. For the sake of example we will say that it is 75 degrees. Place the bottom centre of the protractor on the mark which you have made on the bottom line, follow the 75 degree line up the protractor, and mark your top line where it crosses. Then just draw a line between the two, and you will have the correct angle of your letter. Do this for each letter, and you should have a beautifully even engraving.

This type of lettering looks good on its own, but by embellishing it with flourishes, you can create a complete and intricate design on the goblet, much in demand on presentation pieces.

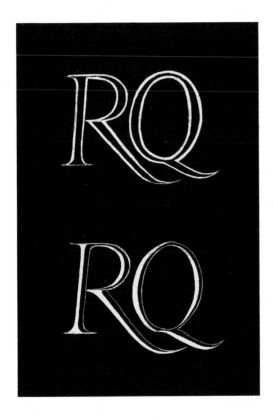

**OUTLINE LETTERING**

*Outline lettering must be executed with great care. In the basic letter, the outline must be of the same thickness all round. For variation, the line on one side of the letter can be thickened.*

51

# Flourishes

Flourishes look beautiful with italic or copperplate lettering, and were much used in the manuscripts of the eighteenth century. They give a feeling of vitality and fun to the work, and are particularly good on glass. They can be used either to enclose the lettering in a defined space, or to dance round the glass, to create an all-round pattern.

Having said all that, they are extremely difficult to design. They must flow in the right direction from the letter involved, and must have the right thick and thin areas in the right places. They must flow out of the letters and not conflict with them in any way, which can be quite difficult to achieve on an all-round design. The message must always be easily read.

When designing flourishes, it is important to realise that their impact on the viewer is not caused by the flourishes alone. The space they enclose is also part of the design (as in all cases of design, whether with lettering or without). It is therefore desirable that the spaces themselves are of an interesting shape, and not all the same, otherwise the design will lose all its excitement.

Flourishes which are independent of the lettering can be used to bind the others together. This is particularly useful when using flourishes to enclose the message in a border. Normally, when designing, one would thicken the stroke at the curve, but this is not always the case and sometimes the stroke is thickened at a different point. Each flourish should be viewed against its neighbour, then it should be easy to see where the thickening of the stroke needs to be.

I find that, when designing flourishes, it is best to do so directly on the glass, so that you can see immediately what the effect is. I use a spirit-based pen to do this. It can take a very long time to achieve the desired effect, and, certainly, the designing takes longer than the actual engraving. Patience is a very useful ingredient.

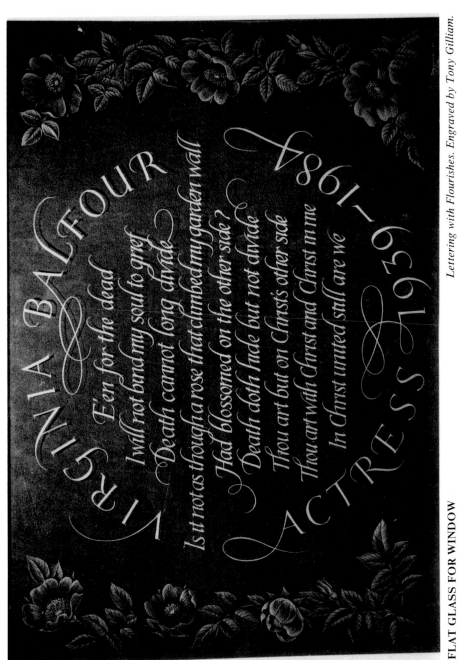

VIRGINIA BALFOUR

E'en for the dead
I will not bind my soul to grief
Death cannot long divide.
Is it not as though a rose that climbed my garden wall
Had blossomed on the other side?
Death doth hide but not divide
Thou art but on Christ's other side
Thou art with Christ and Christ in me
In Christ united still are we

ACTRESS 1939–1984

**FLAT GLASS FOR WINDOW**

*Lettering with Flourishes. Engraved by Tony Gilliam.*

# Cameo Lettering

The technique of this engraving is the cutting away of the background glass, leaving the design standing proud. It is difficult to do, and very slow. Those, who are prepared to spend time on it, however, will be well rewarded.

Cameo lettering is more dramatic when used with block or roman lettering, although the serifs in roman lettering have to be engraved round with great care. When you have designed your letters, and transferred them onto the glass, take a pointed bur and outline them. This must be done to stop them being washed away by the water which you will be using. Be very careful not to chip the glass on the inside of the line, as this is the part which will be standing proud and, if marked or chipped, it will certainly show up clearly.

When this is done, change the bur for a ball-ended or round-edged wheel. The size depends on the areas of engraving which are to be done. Obviously, in small areas, for example, edges of serifs or corners in the lettering background, small heads will have to be used. As with intaglio engraving, the work is done by small circular movements without pressure. A water drip is necessary for this work, first, to aid the speed of cut and to keep the glass cool, and second, because the engraved area must be very smooth. When you have reached the required depth, change the bur for an Arkansas stone (soft white), the same shape and size as the heads which you have been using. Again with small circular strokes, go over the whole engraved area, until it is as even as you can get it, and is semi-transparent. When you have reached this stage you are ready for polishing.

Take one of your cork wheels and get it ready in your drill. Mix up water and pumice powder to a creamy consistency and start to polish. Don't let the glass overheat, or, as explained earlier, it can crack. When the glass is transparent, with just the polishing bloom showing, change to a felt polisher, and, using the cerium oxide and water mix, polish the bloom away. As a final polish, and to get into the small areas, a dental brush can be used in the last stage of polishing.

**CAMEO LETTERING**

*In the case the background has been sandblasted to remove the glass, but the same effect can be achieved by careful cutting with a drill.*
*Engraved by Tony Gilliam.*

# CHAPTER IX

# SAFETY

Various hazards are encountered when engraving, some of which are obvious and some of which are not so obvious. Anyone embarking on this exciting craft must realise that, as in most activities, there are dangers which, once identified and acted upon, are not serious.

The first danger we must discuss is the problem of glass dust. When hand engraving with a diamond point this is so minimal as to be unimportant and can therefore be ignored. When engraving with power tools, however, it becomes a real danger, so that, when surface engraving, a mask should always be worn. The mask ought to be one which is marked with the British Standard kite mark, as being suitable for *fine dust particles*. An ordinary surgical mask, as bought in a pharmacy, or a shaped paper mask, which I have seen some engravers wearing, simply will not do. They give no protection from the very fine dust particles which are ground off the glass.

When doing intaglio or cameo work, it is essential to use water, which, apart from cooling the glass, will wash the dust into the bottom of the tray. When immersed in water ground glass is quite safe as it cannot be breathed in. Under no circumstances must intaglio or cameo cutting be attempted dry, as, not only will the glass overheat, but great clouds of dust will be generated as the wheel grinds off the glass, and this is very dangerous. *Don't forget - glass dust can damage your lungs and respiratory system.*

Next we come to eye protection. In the normal type of engraving there is very little danger to the eyes. However, having said that, many people do seem to get some irritation from glass dust, with red or itchy eyes. If you are one of these unfortunate people, then you should wear goggles or some other form of eye protection. When engraving glass with any amount of tension or stress in it, goggles would also be a wise precaution. The type of glass which could be a danger includes brandy balloons, cullet, and any glass you may suspect of not having been properly anneated. If working in situ, it is always wise to wear a visor which covers the whole face and neck. Accidents rarely happen, but if they do occur on this scale, and you are not protected, the results could be very nasty indeed.

The next word of warning is about a danger which may not be obvious but could be fatal, as I very nearly found out to my cost several years ago. *Never* wear a scarf or tie, or anything around the neck that could get caught up in the rotating drill. If a large drill is being used and something loose around the neck were to get caught in the rotating end of it, strangulation is possible.

The same goes for hair. If you have long hair, plait it or tie it back firmly, so that it cannot get caught in the drill. Having your hair pulled out by the roots would be very painful.

Although etching paste, which can be bought in retail outlets, for glass etching, is relatively safe in adult hands, it is still very toxic. Keep it well out of the reach of children or pets. When using it yourself make sure that you do not inadvertently get it near your mouth or eyes. If you get it on your hands, wash in cool or warm water and all will be well. Do not, however, leave it on your skin longer than is absolutely necessary before washing. Although I have never known it to happen, it could cause a burn.

A final word about safety. When working with water always check beforehand, to make sure that your equipment is double-insulated. Electricity and water are a very dangerous combination, as water is one of the best conductors of electricity known. It is therefore important that you realise this and minimize all possible dangers. The use of fine rubber surgical gloves, while working in these conditions is quite a good idea, but they must be rubber, plastic will not do. I have never heard of an engraving accident caused by this means, so *don't be the first*.

*The contents of this chapter have already been touched on in other parts of this book, but for that I give no apology, as Safety is of paramount importance.*

# CHAPTER X

# SELECTING BLANKS
# FOR ENGRAVING

It is sometimes very difficult for a beginner to find glass blanks which are suitable for engraving. They all too often go out and buy a cheap glass thinking that, to start with, buying a good glass, with some lead content, would be extremely extravagant. This, however, is not the case, and there are several reasons why any old glass will not do. First, the tools which are being used are themselves not cheap. As explained elsewhere in this book, the tools are, in most cases, made of diamond. In hand tools they are brittle, and on burs electroplated onto a shaft. When used on hard glass they wear out very quickly, so buying cheap glass is a false economy.

Secondly hard glass has a greater tendency to chip down the cut line, and is absolutely impossible to engrave successfully. It is therefore impossible to produce a well-engraved piece. As a beginner you need to be able to produce something presentable, otherwise confidence is lost, you will become frustrated, decide that this craft is not for you and give it up almost before you have started. You will never known the joy of producing a magical piece of work, created not by paint and a brush, but with light and a diamond.

## Lead Content

It is often difficult for the inexperienced engraver to tell the difference between glass and crystal, but, in time, you should have some idea by the look and feel of the material.

The majority of shops which sell glass employ assistants who do not know the difference either, so if you go into a shop and ask for a glass with a 24 per cent lead content, it is doubtful if they will be able to help you. This, of course, is the general case; you may be lucky!

Most imported glass now has a small stick-on label which will say 24 per cent. Glass made in England is not generally labelled. If the glass is not labelled you will have to rely on the make. Dartington Glass can be good to work on, and can be bought in most retail shops around the country. Orrefors mark their glass with a red sticker for full-lead crystal and a black sticker for half-lead crystal. However, this crystal is somewhat expensive for a beginner to work on. Kosta Boda is another crystal which is pleasant to work on, but again it is expensive. If you live near a glasshouse, you may be lucky enough to pick up some bargains in their seconds shop. There are several in the Stourbridge area, while Cumbria Crystal, in the Lake District, has a good seconds shop.

## Glass Shapes

Until you become more experienced, stick to straight-sided glass if at all possible. You will be much happier working on this until you have gained confidence.

When looking for glass it is important to choose pieces which are well designed, elegant and with good proportions. Some beautiful baluster goblets are available. There is also some very dull and badly designed glass about. Bowls should be steady and well supported on their feet, with no movement when touched, as this can indicate that they are top heavy or that the foot is warped, and are therefore unsuitable. Good glass should feel quite heavy when it is lifted.

Decanters, whether for wine or spirits, should have a firm, flat base, which should be thicker than the rest of the decanter. This makes for greater stability. Also check to see that the stopper has been ground to the right size. It should fit firmly in the mouth of the decanter, and not move even slightly in any direction when touched. When buying decanters for engraving, it is well to avoid those made with thin glass.

Any very rounded glass is also best avoided, as there is a great deal of tension in it. If you must engrave brandy balloons, only buy those which are of good quality and of thick glass. Even so, wear protective goggles when engraving these, as tensions are unpredictable and the glass might shatter.

There are some beautiful, thick, heavy vases about, and these are perfect when doing intaglio work. A great many of them are straight-sided and therefore easy to work on. Again, check that they stand firmly on their bases, with no slight wobble when touched.

Perfect for the beginner are plates and dishes. These of course, are flat, so you do not even have to worry about working on a curve. The dishes, made in Japan, come in three sizes, small, medium and large. They are octagonal, with a slight lip of about 19 mm. These dishes are 24 per cent lead and are not expensive. The plates vary in price and in quality, and are about the size of tea plates. They are made by various manufacturers, and have different amounts of lead content. Both plates and dishes are available from suppliers mentioned later in this book.

*i. Crystal Box.*

*ii. Goblet*

*iii. Decanter*

*iv. Heavy Crystal Vase*

*v. Selection of paperweights*     *Paperweights are usually suitable for beginners to work on, as they nearly always have one flat surface.*

## Cased and Coloured Glass

It is doubtful that, as a beginner you are likely to use cased or coloured glass, so I will just write a short paragraph about it. Cased glass is used for cameo engraving and also intaglio engraving, when two colours of glass are desirable. Often the colour is layed on clear glass, but of course, a colour can be laid over another colour and could be ordered from the glass blower direct. Flat coloured or cased glass can be bought from stained glass suppliers, but surface engraving does not show up on it very well. Intaglio cutting is satisfactory if the piece is going to be displayed with a light behind it or is going to be put in a window. Flat cased glass is very effective when intaglio-cut for a panel.

One word of warning for those who are going to engrave this glass. It is very, very hard, so both patience and purse are going to be well stretched. The tools will wear out very quickly!

## Flat Glass

Flat glass is very hard to work on and unfortunately it is not possible to buy it with a lead content at the moment. It is, therefore, necessary, when engraving windows or panels, to come to terms with the difficulties before work commences.

First, it is going to take time, so you will have to draw on your reserves of patience. It can take several hours to do a tiny piece of engraving properly. You must also come to terms with the fact that, if you use diamond tools, they are going to wear out at high speed, and this could be costly. Certain measures can be taken to eleviate both these problems, although not to eradicate them completely.

The problem should be tackled from the beginning, at the design stage. Work out a design which is broad-based in conception, with not too much fine detail. By doing this you will then be able to do the engraving with larger stone or composition heads or wheels. This will save some time and a lot of wear and tear on your tools, for although the stone and composition tools wear out too, they are much cheaper to buy. When the majority of the work has been completed, the precious diamond heads can be used for just the detail. In all cases of flat-glass engraving, water should be used as a lubricant, to help both the speed and depth of cutting, and also to protect the glass from overheating. If working in situ, which I try to avoid, I wear a visor which covers my whole face. If the window is going to shatter in this situation, it is going to shatter over you. It is, therefore, just as well to be prepared in case, as is remotely possible, this happens.

If the glass can possibly be engraved in the studio, this is a much better option. You have all your tools round you, in an area you feel comfortable in. You will not need to be on ladders, or scaffolding platforms, and the whole operation is less stressful.

**FLAT 1/4 PLATE GLASS**

*Panel; Apocolypse II. Engraved by the author*

**FLAT 1/4 PLATE GLASS**

*Panel: Ecce Homo. Drill engraved by the author*

# CHAPTER XI

# DISPLAY TECHNIQUES

Engraved glass can be very difficult to display successfully. This is especially true, when stipple engraving is to be displayed, as properly done, it is like a fine mist on the glass, which, without correct lighting, can hardly be seen. It is particularly important, when designing an exhibition, to see that the lighting is adequate and properly placed, and we will touch on this later in the chapter.

## Cabinets: Direct Lighting

When more than one piece of glass is to be displayed in a cabinet, it is obviously better to use direct lighting. For stipple display this is not the solution, but for all other forms of engraving it is quite good.

The cabinet should be made of wood, as this is a natural material and blends well into most surroundings. The inside of the cabinet should be lined with a very dark non-reflective material. I think black is the most dramatic, but many engravers prefer another very dark colour. Cotton velvet is a good lining, but care must be taken to ensure that it does not fray along the edges, as this is very untidy and spoils the display. Another good material is self-adhesive baize, which is much easier to stick on. This can be bought at good hardware and DIY shops, and comes in black and some other colours. This material does not fray, so that problem is eliminated. However, when a glass has been standing in one place for some time and is then moved, it leaves a mark or slight indentation which can be difficult to get rid of.

Now we come to a very important point — the lighting. Two forms of lighting can be used. First, daylight fluorescent tubes, which give a cold, white light. These have the advantage of lighting the whole and should be placed at the top, out of sight of the viewer. If the cabinet is front-opening, they can be attached to the ceiling with a shield in front of them to hide them from the viewer. If a top-loading cabinet is used, they can be placed in the lid. There will probably be a flange round this, which will hide the lights.

The other good type of lighting is halogene spotlights. They can be bought as quite small units, and can be either free-standing in the cabinet, or mounted at the top. If free-standing they should be placed in such a position that they will light the engraving without too much reflection.

Never use a warm-tinted light, as they do not do justice to the engraving, and can make it look flat and uninteresting.

## Indirect Lighting

This is a much more dramatic way to light your engraving, and is a must for stipple work whenever possible.

The cabinets are usually made for a single glass, as it is difficult to light several glasses indirectly in a larger case. The construction of the case is the same as before, wood being the most natural material to use, but these cases are, to the best of my knowledge, always front-loading. There is no lighting in the top of the case, and the glass is either placed on a raised area of the floor, or the case has a false bottom, in which the light is placed. The light is situated facing the back of the cabinet, underneath the false floor or raised area. Opposite the light is a mirror mounted at an angle also under the false floor or behind the raised area. This reflects the light through a slot in the floor, to light the glass from below and behind. This type of lighting makes the engraving look as though it is hovering in space.

Another method of lighting the glass, is to have the light pointing directly through a small hole in the floor, situated under the glass. This has the effect of lighting only the glass and not the background. For both these methods of lighting it is important to have good ventilation and a bulb that does not get hot, as overheating can occur if efforts are not made to avoid it.

## Stands: Incorporating Lighting

If you feel that making a cabinet is more than you can manage, it may be possible for you to make a stand. They are, of course, not as effective as a cabinet for display purposes, but have the advantage of underneath lighting, which helps to enhance the engraving. As with the cabinet, the lighting is hidden in the plinth. Both types of indirect lighting already explained can be used, but again, care must be taken to avoid overheating. The plinth, or box-like structure on which the glass is to stand, should be made of something reasonably light-weight, such as plywood. The back could be left off to help ventilation, but, in this case, a small upwardly angled flap at the back will help the escaping light to be directed away from the glass. The whole stand should be covered in self-adhesive black baize. Cut a hole where the light is to come out, under, or just behind, the glass.

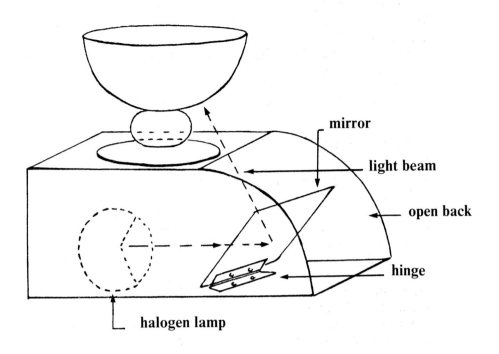

mirror

light beam

open back

hinge

halogen lamp

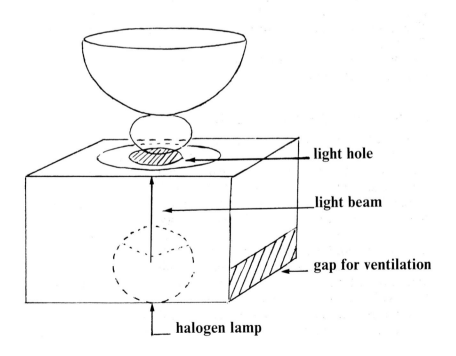

light hole

light beam

gap for ventilation

halogen lamp

## Spotlights

When it is not possible to display your engraving either in a cabinet or on a stand, it is necessary to employ the use of spotlights. The best ones to use for engraved pieces are halogene lights. These issue a very white, bright light, and the spotlights in question could highlight one or two pieces, but not more, as the beam is narrow and concentrated. They should be aimed directly to the side of, or just behind the engraving which is to be illuminated. If they are directed on the front they will produce unwanted reflection, which will detract from the work.

# Designing Your Exhibition

Designing an exhibition takes time. When a suitable venue is found, the floor space should be measured up and then drawn to scale on plan paper. The cases should then also be measured, drawn to scale on card and cut out. These can then be moved about on your own scale model of the floor space, until they are placed in the most interesting positons. They can then be drawn round with pencil and marked permanently on the plan. To go into an exhibition where all the exhibits and cabinets are placed in a straight line against the wall is very dull indeed, and does not tempt the potential visitor to enter the room. The same applies when considering the placing of the glass in the cases. The pieces should be at different heights and small blocks of different heights should be made to support them. These can be made of any firm material and covered in self-adhesive baize. This plan should be followed in the case of joint or group exhibitions as well as one-person shows, as it saves a lot of trauma.

Before setting up the exhibition, it is imperative to walk around the room and see where the light switches and powerpoints are located. The situation of these should also be marked on the plan, as should their height from the floor. You may have to use a multisocket if there are not enough power points, but this not a problem if using halogene spotlights, as they need little electricity.

If you have planned your layout in advance, it should not be too difficult to get the room ready on the day. The stipple glass pieces should be in cases in some part of the room which is dark, or can be darkened, so that they show up well. Surface engraving should be in the other cases, and spotlights can be used to light bowls and panels which can be placed on tables.

If you wish to sell your work, check with the venue in advance. Such places as museums frequently do not allow you to sell from their premises, and it can create an awkward situation if you do not know this beforehand.

If you decide to have a preview, check that you can bring food onto the premises yourself or whether the authorities responsible for the building expect you to use their caterers, which can push the price up considerably. The same goes for wine. The authorities may insist that they supply it or they may charge a corkage fee on each bottle you bring onto their premises. The whole thing, of course, may be unrestricted, but you need to know all these points well ahead of time.

**GLASS ON DISPLAY**

*Note that some glass is raised to make display more interesting.*
*Photo by Diana Newnes*

# APPENDICES

# GUILD OF GLASS ENGRAVERS

All those who embark on the task of learning the craft of glass engraving, will find the Guild of Glass Engravers a source of much help and encouragement. The guild can also put you in touch with their local branches, who have a comprehensive programme of lectures, visits, exhibitions and workdays. The members are always happy to welcome and help newcomers, and meetings are always very convivial occasions. There are branches in East Anglia, the Chilterns, Oxford, the South West and Sussex (which draws its membership also from the nearer borders of Hampshire and Kent). In addition, there is a Scottish Glass Society which covers a range of glass crafts. The Guild of Glass Engravers would probably be able to give you other useful addresses.

Contact should be made with the Guild of Glass Engravers by writing to:

Katherine Coleman
Sec. Guild of Glass Engravers
49 Crediton Hill,
London NW6 1HS
Tel: 081-794 0644

(available weekdays: 2 p.m. - 5 p.m.
on Thursdays: 2 p.m. - 8 p.m.)

# PHOTOGRAPHY

Photographing one's work is always a problem. To have it photographed professionally is very expensive. The main problem with doing it oneself is that most reflections and highlights have to be eliminated, if the engraving is to be seen properly, and this is not easy.

The first thing to consider is the background. The engraving is white, so black or a very dark colour of background is best to give as much contrast as possible. The best material to use is cotton velvet, which has a minimum reflective surface. Nylon velvet is not so good, as it has a slight sheen and therefore reflects more light. It is best to drape the material over a hard chair, so that there is no obvious 'back' or 'floor' to the photograph. Successful photographs can be taken in strong sunlight, but here I have explained how to take them indoors, as then one is not reliant on the weather.

For this type of photography, a single lens reflex camera is needed. This is because what you see in the viewfinder is what you get in the photograph, and there is a deal of trial and error in arranging everything correctly.

A tripod is necessary to hold the camera completely still when you have found the right position for it. I also have two photo flood lights, but often only use one of them. It is a good idea to eliminate all background light, so that you can move the photo floods around until no serious reflections show up on the engraved parts of the glass. It is helpful to have a polarized filter over the lens of your camera, as this also helps to reduce reflection. These can be bought in camera shops to fit most SLR cameras.

Make sure that the glass is really clean, as any tiny speck of dust or fingerprint will show up under the very bright light. Place the glass on the velvet, making sure that it is on a very firm base. Now place the camera on the tripod in front of it, and check through the viewfinder to see what the glass looks like. If there are reflections, move the lights or try only one. There is a great deal of trial and error in this process, and one must check through the viewfinder at every point until satisfied with the result.

Having experimented and arrived at a picture in the viewfinder which is pleasing, it is then necessary to check the aperture and exposure time required for the speed of film which is being used. It is best to keep the exposure time to below one second if possible, as many things can move far enough in that time to lose the crispness of the photograph.

Having checked everything once, it should be checked again. It is very disappointing to find a fault in the finished photograph, which could easily have been avoided if only it had been noticed in time, and often one may not have the chance to photograph the piece again. Once a good picture has been taken, it is worth while to be bold and have it printed in a large size.

# SUPPLIERS OF
# TOOLS AND EQUIPMENT·

Tools and equipment for glass engraving are not readily available at general craft shops, so it is often necessary to write away for supplies. Dental suppliers will be able to supply burs and drills, but very few of them will be able to give you any practical advice as regards to the use of the tools they sell (for glass engraving purposes, that is). They do not, of course, sell some of the specialist tools which you may need.

The following addresses are useful when trying to track down suppliers:

B H Specialist Services
87, Corportation Road
Grangetown
Cardiff CF1 7AQ
Tel: 0222-231183

Comprehensive suppliers of a wide range of tools for both hand and power engraving. These include, craft drills, diamond burs, tungsten carbide points, rubber polishers inpregnated with abrasive, sintered diamonds glass paperweights, Austrian crystal pendant, glass domes, wooden bases and etching paste. They also supply an economically priced micromotor (foot and hand switch interchangeable, speed variable, control by dial on front of box and forward/reverse action).

FCA/SECO
414, Oakleigh Road North
Whetstone
London N20 0R7
Tel: 01-368-4649

Suppliers of pendant drills. These drills are manufactured on the premises, including the motor which runs them.

FCA took over Terence Long, who were the manufacturers of the SECO drill, some 24 months ago, and now have a new flexishaft pendant drill available. This has a 5-mm inner cable for strength, and has a very subtle drive, which makes it easy to use. They will soon be producing an electronic control which will be usable with existing foot controls.

Micromotor with slip joint fitting for separate handpieces also available.

A D Burs
10/11 Madleaze Estate
Bristol Road
Gloucester GL1 5SG
Tel: 0452-306105
Telex: 43103
Fax: 0452-300799

Manufacturers and suppliers of a comprehensive range of tools: diamond points, tungsten carbide points, diamond files, polishing brushes, abrasive points, tungsten carbide hand tools, impregnated polishing heads, specialist diamond plating facility. Distributors of sintered burs and other rotary products.

Quayle Dental MFG Co Ltd
Derotor House
Domonion Way
Worthing
West Sussex
BN14 8QN
Tel: 0903-204427
Telex: 878336 Quayle G
Fax: 0903-212848

Manufacturers and suppliers of Derotor craft tools and pendant motors. Flexible drive shafts manufactured to suit most types of motor, with either a fixed or detachable handpieces. Bench support stands, handpieces, burs, and abrasives, micromotors of various speeds and styles. The factory at Worthing has a comprehensive service department to handle all motors servicing and also repairs of all makes of motor or handpieces.

Sunshine Farm Crafts
Hilton Lane
Essington
Wolverhampton
WV11 2AU
Tel: 0922-416948

Collection of glassware from 11 different countries, especially concentrating on paperweights. This company caters for the small craftsperson and has a wide range of blanks, from full lead crystal through the spectrum to plain glass.
Available by mail order and there is no stipulation on minimum orders. Colour brochure on request.

John Jenkins and Sons Ltd
Nyewood Rogate
Petersfield
Hants
Tel: (shop) Rogate 495

Importers of glass and crystal. Large variety of blanks of all qualities. Good range of lead crystal. When buying from the warehouse it is necessary to have an account with them, and for this there is a minimum order. However, they have a very good shop on their premises which is open to the public, and has a good selection of firsts, seconds and discontinued ranges. For this there is no minimum order.

Dexam International Ltd
Haslemere
Surrey
Warehouse:
  Holmbush Way
Midhurst
West Sussex

Importers of high quality crystal. Distributors for Orrefors and Kosta Boda. They are primarily, a wholesale distributor to the trade, but have a very good seconds shop at their premises at Midhurst, which opens on two mornings a week.

Neil Wilkin Glass
Dartington Glassworks
Torrington
Devon EX38 7AN
Tel: 0805-23528

Mouth-blown glass to commission. Maker of cased glass in transparent or opaque metal.
Can be commissioned by individuals or groups, who can book one, two or three days' glass production. Sometimes has glass for sale in stock.

# GLOSSARY

**Annealing**  The tempering of glass by controlled heat and gradual cooling to prevent stress.

**Arrissing**  The process of removing sharp edges from glass.

**Blanks**  Plain glass shapes and vessels, to be used for engraving, etching or other forms of decoration.

**Burnish**  To rub down firmly the edges of a stencil, so that acid does not leak underneath it.

**Cameo**  i)  A glass gem or vessel where a layer of coloured glass is flashed onto another layer of glass which can be plain or coloured. The background glass is then cut away in different amounts to show the design. (Example: The Portland vase which can be seen at the British Museum).
ii)  Relief carving.

**Chuck**  Another name for a collet

**Clear Acid**  Hydroflouric acid which gives a clear etch. Dangerous in use as it causes severe burns.

**Collet**  Small metal grips which hold the engraving points firmly in the end of the drill.

**Crosshatch**  Lines in one direction crossed by lines in another direction.

**Diamond Bur**  A steel shaft with diamond dust bonded onto it, often by electroplating.

**Diamond point engraving**  Hand decoration of glass with a diamond.

**Embossing Black**  A black acid-resistant paint

**Engraving**  Decoration by means of hand tools or power tools. These include, diamond point, tungsten carbide point, diamond bur, diamond wheel and copper wheel.

**Etching**  A process by which the glass is decorated by the use of acids.

| | |
|---|---|
| **Flashing** | The process in which glass of one colour is covered by a thin layer of glass in a different colour. |
| **Flexible Shaft** | A long shaft attached to a motor so that the rotating end can be used away from the motor. |
| **Glass House** | A factory where glass is made. |
| **Intaglio** | Engraving cut deeply into the glass. |
| **Lehr** | A long tunnel-like structure in which molten glass is slowly cooled to anneal it. |
| **Mandrel** | Shaft on which polishing cones, discs and diamond wheels can be fixed. Sometimes called an arbor or spindle. |
| **Metal** | A term used by glass makers for glass. |
| **Mica** | French chalk which can be mixed with embossing black to make an acid-resistant stencil. |
| **Pin Vice** | Adjustable holder to take engraving points. |
| **Polishing discs and cones** | Cones and discs which are made of rubber impregnated with grit or silicone to be used for basic polishing. |
| **Pumice** | Fine abrasive powder for polishing glass. |
| **Resist** | Any material which prevents acid from attacking glass. |
| **Sand box** | Box filled with sand. The middle can be hollowed out to hold glass whilst work is in progress.<br>There must be adequate protection to prevent the sand from scratching the glass.<br>A safer alternative would be a black cushion filled with polyeurethane chips. |
| **Scalpel** | A very sharp surgical knife with replaceable blades. |
| **Scratchy** | A term used for the uneven cutting of a line, usually slight chipping along its edges. |
| **Shape** | A blank with a curved surface. |

| | |
|---|---|
| **Sintered Bur** | Bur, on which the diamond dust has been bonded to the matrix at high temperature. These have a longer life than ordinary burs. |
| **Stipple** | A form of engraving produced by diamond or tungsten hand tools, in which the design is built up by gently tapping the tool against the glass, to produce a series of small dots. |
| **Torque** | Turning capacity of drill under pressure. |
| **White Acid** | Hydrofluoric acid with a bifluoride additive which gives a frosted etch. Dangerous to use, causes severe burns. |
| **Working Drawings** | Term used for a drawing on which all working instructions are marked pictorially. |